♌ Leo

♎ Libra

♏ Scorpius

♐ Sagittarius

♑ Capricornus

First published in Great Britain 1984 by
Webb and Bower (Publishers) Limited
9 Colleton Crescent, Exeter, Devon EX2 4BY

Edited, designed and illustrated by
the E.T. Archive Limited
Chelsea Wharf, 15 Lots Road, London SW10 0QH

Designed by Julian Holland
Picture Research by Anne-Marie Ehrlich
Special photography by Eileen Tweedy
Copyright © text and illustrations E.T. Archive Ltd 1984

British Library Cataloguing in Publication Data

Parker, Julia
  Signs of the zodiac.—(A Webb & Bower miniature)
  1. Zodiac—Pictorial works
  I. Title
  133.5'2'0222   BF1726

  ISBN 0–86350–013–7

Phototypeset by Text Filmsetters Limited, Orpington, Kent
Printed and bound in Hong Kong by Mandarin Offset International Limited

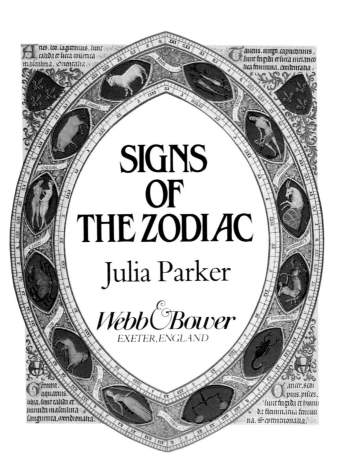

SIGNS
OF
THE ZODIAC

Julia Parker

Webb & Bower
EXETER, ENGLAND

Aries

21 March–20 April

The glyph of the sign (♈) represents the horns of the ram. Its ruling planet is Mars. This sign is positive and masculine, and therefore extrovert. Its element is fire, and it is a cardinal sign, and so outgoing. Its body area is the head. The Arian metal is iron, its gemstone, diamond, and its colour, red. The Arian flower is honeysuckle, and all thorn-bearing trees come under its influence. Arian spices are mustard and cayenne pepper, and its foodstuffs, onions, leeks and hops. The creatures it governs are sheep and rams. The countries of England, France and Germany are ruled by Aries, as are the cities of Naples, Florence, Crakow and Birmingham (UK).

There was famine in Boeotia. Ino bore a grudge against her stepchildren and bribed the Oracle at Delphi to say that the crops would only flourish again if King Athamas, her husband, sacrificed his handsome son by his previous marriage, Phrixus, to Zeus. As Athamas was about to make the sacrifice, Zeus sent to the rescue a magnificent ram with a golden fleece and wings. Phrixus and his sister Helle climbed onto the ram's back and flew off to Colchis, but Helle lost her grip and fell into the straits between Europe and Asia – the Hellespont. On his arrival, Phrixus sacrificed the ram to Zeus, and the fleece was hung in the Temple of Ares at Colchis, where the Argonauts came in search of it. Ares, the war-like son of Hera and Zeus, had many Arian characteristics.

Aries is the first sign of the Zodiac, marking the beginning of the astrological New Year – so Arians must be leaders, pioneers who must also win. 'Me first!' is their cry. Their motivation is simple, straightforward and uncluttered; they need plenty of freedom of expression to do what they want in their own individual way. Positive and optimistic in outlook, they can achieve a great deal once their ample enthusiasm is ignited and maintained. Their worst fault is selfishness, and they can be careless, especially over details (which they find boring). Arians are decisive and even in really important matters the snap decision is usually the right one. They are prone to headaches (or never get any!) and in undue haste can often cut or burn themselves. Children of this sign are extremely forthright, but need to be encouraged to help with younger brothers and sisters. Provided they can control their selfishness, Arians make excellent partners. Enthusiastic in love and sex, they like to keep their relationships lively and continually developing; their partners may find them demanding, but will never be bored. They are ambitious and need plenty of challenge. If their daily work is repetitive, they must develop demanding spare-time interests.

Taurus

21 April–21 May

The glyph of the sign (♉) represents the horns of the bull. The ruling planet is Venus. The sign is negative and feminine, and therefore introvert. Its element is earth. It is a fixed sign, so Taureans tend to be stubborn. Its body area is the neck and throat. The Taurus metal is copper, the metal of Venus. Its gemstone is emerald and its colour, pink. Taurean flowers are roses, poppies and foxgloves, and its trees, ash, cypress, apple and the vine. Cloves, sorrel and spearmint are Taurean herbs, and its foodstuffs are wheat, berries, apples, pears and grapes. Cattle are its creatures, while countries ruled by Taurus are Ireland, Switzerland and Iran, and its cities are Dublin, Lucerne, Mantua and Leipzig.

Zeus fell in love with Europa, the daughter of Agenor, and persuaded his son Hermes to drive Agenor's cattle down to the sea-shore of Canaan where Zeus disguised himself as a white bull. Europa was attracted to this beautiful beast and made garlands of flowers for him. She climbed onto his back, and he sprang into the sea and swam off with her. He waded ashore at Crete, turned himself into an eagle and raped her. Zeus set the constellation of Taurus in the sky to commemorate this event. In Christian imagery the bull symbol is also that of St Luke.

Taurus, the bull, is steadfast and reliable. Here is a group of people who are loving and passionate, and enjoy the good things of life. They need above-average security, both financial and emotional, as a background to their lives. Once they have this, they will make progress and achieve much. They love luxury and comfort, and their expensive tastes will demand a high salary. In pursuit of this it is too easy for them to become slaves to routine. They are persistent and practical, cautious and have plenty of common sense. Their worst fault is possessiveness. They love to own beautiful things and derive great pleasure from them, and this tends to apply to their partners: If they are not careful they will think of a lover as just one more possession, which can cause difficulties in their relationships. Slow to be aroused, they can show violent temper at times. They are prone to sore throats and loss of voice. As the throat is a Taurean body area, Taureans are often fine singers. They also have a great love of beauty and art. Children of this sign should be encouraged to share their toys with friends and younger brothers and sisters, and must be allowed to develop at their own rate – which can be rather slow. But their power of retention is good. Taureans have a natural business sense, and do extremely well in banking, and working for large organizations.

Gemini

22 May–21 June

The glyph of the sign (♊) represents the heavenly twins. Its ruling planet is Mercury, and it is positive and masculine, and therefore extrovert. Its element is air. It is a mutable sign, so Geminians are flexible. Its body areas are the shoulders, arms and hands. The Geminian metal is mercury, and its gemstone agate. Its colour is yellow. The Geminian flower is lily of the valley and all nut-bearing trees are attributed to the sign. Its herbs are aniseed, caraway and marjoram, and the foodstuffs it rules are nuts, those vegetables which grow above ground, and carrots. Small birds (especially parrots) are governed by Gemini; so are monkeys. Its countries are Wales, Belgium and the USA, and cities coming under its rulership are London, Plymouth (UK), Cardiff, San Francisco and Melbourne.

Castor and Pollux were the brave, handsome twin sons of Leda, but had different fathers. Castor was son of Tyndareus, King of Sparta, while Pollux was son of Zeus. Inseparable, the boys became known as the Dioscuri. Castor was killed in battle. Zeus offered Pollux immortality if he left his mortal brother. This Pollux declined unless his twin could share it with him. Zeus consequently allowed them to spend half their time in the heavens and the other half in the underworld, and rewarded their brotherly love by setting their image in the night sky.

Gemini–twins–duality: here is versatility and liveliness, people who have as many facets as a well-cut gemstone. Geminians must communicate, and will make their opinions known by writing to the newspapers, taking part in 'phone-ins, or just chatting to strangers at every opportunity. Geminians cannot do one thing at a time: that would be boring, and boredom is something every Geminian dreads and even fears. Geminians have excellent minds, and are stimulating company. They like to be kept very busy, but should develop consistency of effort, since in their need to express themselves in a variety of ways they have a strong tendency to leave a trail of unfinished tasks or hobbies behind them. They can talk themselves dextrously out of any tricky situation. They have a high level of nervous energy, and can become restless and sometimes tense. Children of this sign need plenty of intellectual challenge, and must not be allowed to bluff their way through school – all questions must be thoroughly answered. Geminians need partners who enjoy a varied sex-life, can be intellectually stimulating and who value real friendship within an emotional relationship. Geminians flourish in all branches of the media, or in telecommunications. They make excellent salespeople, agents and receptionists.

13

Cancer

22 June–22 July

The glyph of the sign (♋) represents the breasts. Its ruling planet is the Moon. The sign is negative and feminine and so introvert. Its element is water, and it is a cardinal sign, therefore outgoing. Its body areas are the chest and breasts. Its metal is silver and its gemstone, pearls, its colour, silver-grey. The flowers it rules are acanthus, convolvulus, and white flowers in general. The trees are those rich in sap, while its herbs are saxifrage, verbena and tarragon. Its food-stuffs are milk, fish, and fruits and vegetables with a high water content. Cancer rules creatures with a hard shell or skin. Its countries are Scotland and Holland, and its cities Manchester (UK), Amsterdam, Tokyo and New York.

The myth of Cancer arose in Babylon, but in Egypt the constellation was sometimes represented by two turtles – known as the Stars of the Water – and sometimes by an unidentified water creature, Allul. One of Heracles' twelve labours was to defeat the Hydra, a watersnake with many heads. Each time Heracles cut off a head another two grew in its place. Hera sent an enormous crab to help the Hydra. It attacked Heracles but was crushed and eventually overcome by him. In gratitude for his efforts against Heracles, Hera promoted the crab to heaven.

Cancer the crab is the sensitive, protective one whose intuition and emotions are abundant and whose imagination and memory are second to none. Cancerians defend themselves and their principles. If Cancerians are challenged in argument, they are naturally and instantly on the defensive, and they also protect and cherish loved ones in a very special way. Cancerian moods are as changeable as the phases of the Moon (their ruling planet), and they are extremely sensitive. They are very prone to worry, and should use their marvellous intuition to counter this. They are easily hurt, but may also hurt others more than they think. They are eager to have their own home and family, and will establish them as soon as possible; family life is important to them, and they are often upset when their children grow up and leave home. Cancerian children are imaginative and make caring brothers and sisters, but they must not be allowed to be clinging or over-cautious. Cancerians are sensual lovers, but both sexes must be careful not to smother their partners in a maternal way. Here are the best cooks in the Zodiac. Many make excellent children's nurses, historians, antique dealers and collectors, and will thrive in any profession in which they can express their imagination and caring, protective instincts.

Leo

The glyph of the sign (Ω) represents the lion's tail. The ruling planet is the Sun, and the sign is positive and masculine, therefore extrovert. Its element is fire and it is a fixed sign, so Leos tend to be stubborn. Its body areas are the heart and spine, its metal, gold and its gemstone, ruby, its colours are those of the Sun, from sunrise to sunset. Leo flowers are sunflowers and marigolds; palms, oranges, lemons and laurels are its trees. Leo herbs are saffron, rosemary and peppermint; rice, and honey are its foodstuffs. Its creatures are big game, especially the cat family. Countries under its rulership are Italy, Romania, Sicily and the south of France. Leo cities are Rome, Prague, Bombay, Madrid, Philadelphia, Chicago, Los Angeles, Bath and Bristol.

The first labour imposed by Eurystheus on Heracles was the killing of an enormously powerful lion, invulnerable to weapons of stone, iron or bronze. Heracles eventually overcame it by strangling it and Zeus placed it in the sky. Two Greek gods are associated with the Sun myth: Apollo, who was superior to Pan in the art of piping and so became god of music, and Helios, who each morning harnessed his winged horses and rode across the vault of heaven shedding light on men and gods alike. At night, while his horses were pastured in the Islands of the Blest, he slept in his chariot as it was ferried on a golden ship through the underworld. The lion is also the symbol of the Christian evangelist St Mark.

The lion is the king of the animals, and all Leos will see to it that they have their own individual kingdom, large or small. Here is fiery enthusiasm in plenty, optimism and a natural ability to do everything in a big and impressive way. Leos have a great sense of drama, and will make the simplest event a memorable occasion. There is creative power and potential in every Leo, and it is up to the individual to find a way of expressing it, not necessarily in art, though there are many Leo artists, dancers, painters and actors. Leos are big-hearted and magnanimous, but bossiness is their worst fault, and they will all too readily take over the management of other people's lives, believing that they can cope far better. The Leo body areas are the heart and spine, and it is important for them to exercise both regularly. Their taste is excellent, but very expensive – only the best will do. Children of this sign need positive encouragement to spur their natural enthusiasm, but must not be allowed to show off too much. Leos love deeply and passionately, but must curb any tendency to dominate their partners, from whom they may sometimes tend to expect too much. Leos need a career in which they can express their superb organizing ability, and one in which they can in some way take the centre of the stage.

Virgo

24 August–22 September

The glyph of the sign (♍) represents the female genitalia. Its ruling planet is Mercury. The sign is negative and feminine, therefore introvert. Its element is earth and it is a mutable sign, so Virgoans are adaptable. The body areas are the stomach and bowels, the metal is mercury or nickel; the gemstone is sardonyx, and the colours, navy blue and dark browns and greens. Small, brightly-coloured flowers such as anemone are attributed to Virgo, and it shares with Gemini the rulership of nut-bearing trees. Virgoan herbs are those which blossom in blue or yellow, and its foodstuffs are vegetables grown under the earth. The sign rules all creatures which can be domestic pets, and Virgo countries are Greece, the West Indies, Turkey, the state of Virginia in the USA, Brazil and New Zealand. The cities it rules are Boston, Paris, Heidelberg and Athens.

The Babylonians first personified Virgo as the grain-goddess Ishtar, or Shala of Sumeria, when the constellation was called *absu*, or furrow. Some think of her as Demeter, the corn-goddess of Eleusis, or her daughter Persephone. She is also known as Dike, who having failed to persuade men of the errors of their ways, forsook them for heaven. Erigone, daughter of Icarius, hanged herself and was immortalized as Virgo after discovering that her father had been accidentally killed by country people intoxicated by wine given to them by Dionysus.

23

Here, with the Virgin, is natural modesty and a certain charming and unaffected shyness. The Virgoan will serve others, if necessary making considerable sacrifices to do so. Here is the busiest and probably the most hard-working of all Zodiac groups. Virgoans have an extremely high level of nervous energy which must be released. If it is not, they will suffer from nervous tension, stomach upsets or perhaps migraine. Their powers of organization are not good; it is better for them to know precisely what is expected of them; they flourish best within a set structure. They can come to terms with worry by approaching problems in a logical and practical way, using their remarkable analytic and critical faculties to the full. But it is this critical streak that can become their worst fault, causing them to nag at times. Restlessness, too, must be countered. Virgoan children are usually popular at school, helpful to teachers and careful and neat in their work. They need to have plenty of stimulating hobbies outside school. Virgoans are sometimes rather reticent in the expression of love and sex, and need stable, sound partners who will develop the friendly, intellectual side of the relationship. They make excellent teachers, work well in the media, horticulture and fringe-medicine. They are also marvellous secretaries and personal assistants.

Libra

23 September–23 October

The glyph of the sign (♎) represents the scales. Its ruling planet is Venus. It is positive and masculine, therefore extrovert. Its element is air, and it is a cardinal sign, therefore outgoing. Its body area is the kidneys. The Libran metal is copper, the metal of Venus, and its gemstone is sapphire. Its colours are shades of pale blue, pink and green. Libran flowers are blue, such as hydrangeas, and its trees are ash and poplar. Its herbs are mint, arrach and its spice, cayenne; its foodstuffs are tomato, asparagus and beans. Its creatures are small reptiles and lizards, and the countries under its rulership are Austria, Burma, Japan, Argentina, Upper Egypt and Canada. Its cities are Copenhagen, Vienna, Johannesburg, Lisbon, Frankfurt and Nottingham.

The constellation was first recognized as early as 2000 BC by the Babylonians, and connected with the judgement of the living and the dead by Zibanitu, the Scales who weighed the souls. The sun is in Libra during the harvest, the time of the weighing of corn and assessment of taxes, but the actual origin of the sign's name is uncertain. In Egyptian mythology it is Osiris who weighs the souls in the scales. Another possible explanation of the scales is that they represent the exact balance of the lengths of day and night at the autumnal equinox at which time the Sun is in Libra.

People of this sign must necessarily share their lives with a sympathetic and understanding partner. The need for balance and harmony is paramount, and they will not become psychologically whole until a happy partnership is achieved. Sometimes their desire for it is so strong that they rush into marriage or a long-term relationship with someone unsuitable, and suffer the consequences. Because they love a peaceful life, they will put up with a lot before taking action. Conversely, they will sometimes purposely 'rock the boat' in order to be reassured of their partner's love – it is so nice when the squabble is made up and they can fall in love all over again! Their worst fault is indecision: 'let us wait and see what happens', can be a too familiar motto. Resentfulness is also common. There are sometimes headaches, perhaps due to slight kidney disorders. Libran children have as much charm and social grace as their elders, but need gentle, firm correction. Librans are successful in the luxury and beauty trades, making excellent managers; diplomatic by nature, we find them working in embassies and in the Army which can also make an attractive, rewarding career for them.

Scorpio

24 October–22 November

The glyph of the sign (♏) represents the male genitalia. Its ruling planet is Pluto, and it is a negative and feminine sign, therefore introvert. Its element is water, and it is a fixed sign, so Scorpios tend to be stubborn. Its body area is the genitals; its metal is steel or iron, and its gemstone opal. Its colours are dark red and maroon, and the flowers it rules are geraniums and rhododendrons. Blackthorn and all bushy trees come under the sign's dominance, and its herbs are aloes, witch-hazel and catmint; its foodstuffs, most strong-tasting foods. Creatures owing their rulership to Scorpio are crustaceans and insects, and its countries are Morocco, Norway, the Transvaal in South Africa and Algeria; its cities are New Orleans, Fez, Milwaukee, Liverpool, Halifax (UK) and Hull.

Artemis, Apollo's sister, was attracted to Orion the Hunter. Fearful of his sister's virtue, Apollo arranged for Orion to be attacked by a huge scorpion, which the handsome hero fought with sword and arrows to no avail. He was forced to dive into the sea to avoid its sting. Artemis, a magnificent shot, put an arrow through the bobbing black head in the water, then discovered she had killed Orion by mistake. Grief-stricken, she placed him as a constellation in the heavens, forever pursued by the scorpion. Scorpio was sometimes represented as an eagle, the symbol of St John the Evangelist.

Scorpio is the strongest and most powerful of all the Zodiac signs, and Scorpios have emotional and physical resources second to none. They must be consciously aware of their power, and recognize that they need to direct their energy in positive and rewarding ways. They need fulfilling work and a strong sense of purpose and direction in life. If they do not have a career which means a great deal to them, it is absolutely vital that they have some really compelling outside interest, otherwise they will stagnate and become unfulfilled and may suffer serious psychological problems. They should develop the capacity to talk over their problems with other people; this is difficult, but important to them. Much is written about Scorpios' high sexuality, and it is of course important that this sphere of their life should be as rewarding and fulfilling as any other, but it is possible for them to direct their formidable sexual energy in other ways. They can become jealous, causing their partners and themselves considerable unhappiness. Children of this sign should be kept very busy and encouraged to take an active interest in sport or in a subject which calls for concentrated effort. Because of an intense desire to get to the root of problems, Scorpios make superb researchers and detectives. Many are successful analysts, wine experts and engineers.

Sagittarius

23 November–21 December

The glyph of the sign (♐) represents the centaur's arrow. Its ruling planet is Jupiter. The sign is positive and masculine, so extrovert. Its element is fire, and it is mutable so Sagittarians are adaptable. Its body areas are the hips, thighs and liver; its metal tin, its gemstone topaz. The Sagittarian colours are dark blues and purple, and its flowers are pinks and carnations. Its trees are limes, birches, mulberries and oaks, and herbs coming under its influence are sage, aniseed and balsam. The foodstuffs attributed to it are bulb vegetables, grapefruit, currants and sultanas. Its creatures are horses and all hunted animals. Countries ruled by it are Spain, Australia, Hungary, South Africa, and its cities are Toledo, Stuttgart, Budapest, Cologne, Sheffield and Washington DC.

Philyra, trying to escape from Kronos, Zeus' father, turned herself into a mare, and Kronos in turn adopted the form of a stallion. When their son was born he proved to be half-man, half-horse. Disgusted at the sight of the little monster, Philyra prayed to be released from nursing him, and was turned into a linden tree. But the baby, Chiron, grew up to be one of the great tutors of ancient times, rearing and educating such heroes as Jason and Achilles, teaching them to hunt with bow and arrow and feeding them on the entrails of lions and on honeycombs to make them brave and give them sweetness of temperament. He also became king of the centaurs and was promoted to the sky by Zeus after renouncing his immortality.

Freedom is essential to Sagittarians: anything savouring of restriction, a room without a view, or a possessive partner, will be disastrous. Sagittarians have considerable versatility, which must be controlled, otherwise the archer of the Zodiac will loose off far too many arrows in all directions, and hit no satisfactory targets. Challenge is vital, so a balance must be achieved. Especially when very young, Sagittarians can be 'coltish' and over-exuberant, and as there is an element of the eternal student about them, it is important that they develop properly from immature student to sage philosopher, and, like the centaur of the myth, become both wise man and adventurous hunter. Enthusiasm and optimism abound and both are infectious. Sagittarians make lively partners but need a good intellectual rapport with their lovers. Restlessness and blind optimism are their worst faults. The hips and thighs are vulnerable, and women of the sign tend to put on weight in these areas. Liverishness can be a problem – Sagittarians love good food and drink. Sagittarian children need plenty of encouragement, but must not be allowed to become too wild. Many of this sign are successful in the law, the church and publishing. Teaching in further education is rewarding, as are the travel and export industries, since there is often a flair for languages.

Capricorn

22 December–20 January

The glyph of the sign (♑) represents the goat's head and its fish tail. Its ruling planet is Saturn, the sign is negative and feminine, therefore introvert. Its element is earth and it is cardinal and therefore outgoing. Its body areas are the knees and shins; skin, teeth and bones also come under its rulership. Its metal is lead, and its gemstones, turquoise and amethyst. Its colours are dark grey and black. Capricorn flowers are ivy, hemlock, medlar and heart's-ease. Its trees are yew, pine and elm. Its herbs are hemp, comfrey and knapweed. Its foodstuffs are potatoes, barley, beet, spinach and malt, and the creatures ruled by it are goats and all cloven-hoofed animals. Its countries are India, Mexico and Afghanistan, and its cities are Oxford (UK), Delhi, Mexico City and the administrative areas of all capital cities.

The mythological associations of Capricorn are uncertain; there are references to Pan, whose mother rejected him because of his ugliness, but who subsequently had great success in seducing nymphs. An ancient Babylonian god called Ea was known as the antelope of the subterranean ocean; the fish-tailed goat was also called *kusarikku*, the fish-ram. The Roman feast of Saturnalia took place at the time when the Sun entered Capricorn – a time of celebration and merry-making which became the Christian festival of Christmas.

Capricorn is the sure-footed goat, climbing further and further up the mountain, knowing precisely where he is going and how he is going to get there. At least, that is the best side of Capricorn. But too often the aspiring ambitious Capricorn can be depressed, negative in outlook – a poor, tethered domestic animal lacking self-confidence. Tradition is important to Capricorns, who are often motivated by a tendency to social climbing. They like to impress others, and appreciate quality in all things. They are cautious, practical, often somewhat reserved and serious in outlook, but mostly with a marvellous sense of humour which is off-beat and very dry. Their caution can lead them to express their worst faults: coldness, meanness and an aptitude for grumbling. They should be teased out of this. They are prone to rheumatic pains, with the knees and shins especially vulnerable, as are their teeth and bones. But they have superb skin and beautiful legs. Capricorn children are serious and determined, and should be encouraged to develop self-confidence. In love, Capricorns are faithful once committed, but sometimes, because of their ambitions and aspirations, concentrate so much on their careers and objectives that they neglect their partners. Musical talent is often present, and many do well in business, as civil servants, as osteopaths or dentists, and in politics or science.

Aquarius

21 January–18 February

The glyph of the sign (♒) represents the waves of water pouring from the water-carrier's jar. The ruling planet is Uranus, the sign is positive and masculine, therefore extrovert. Its element is air, and it is fixed. The body area is the ankles, and circulation is also ruled by the sign. Its metal is aluminium, and its gemstone, aquamarine. Its colour is turquoise, and the flowers it rules are golden rod and the orchid. Its trees are fruit trees and its herbs those with a sharp or unusual flavour. Aquarian creatures are birds with the ability to make long flights, and the countries it rules are the USSR and Sweden; its cities are Moscow, Salzburg, Hamburg and Leningrad.

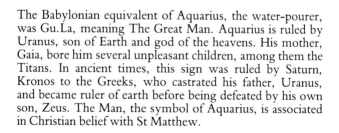

The Babylonian equivalent of Aquarius, the water-pourer, was Gu.La, meaning The Great Man. Aquarius is ruled by Uranus, son of Earth and god of the heavens. His mother, Gaia, bore him several unpleasant children, among them the Titans. In ancient times, this sign was ruled by Saturn, Kronos to the Greeks, who castrated his father, Uranus, and became ruler of earth before being defeated by his own son, Zeus. The Man, the symbol of Aquarius, is associated in Christian belief with St Matthew.

Aquarians are the individualists of the Zodiac, needing total freedom of expression. They are idealistic, original, inventive, and good friends who will do everything they can to help others. The humanitarian qualities of Aquarians are renowned, and they are forward-looking and mix easily with all ages and social groups. But they are also unconventional, private people, who in spite of their friendliness often set a certain distance between themselves and the rest of us. Their worst faults are unpredictability, a tendency to be fixed in their opinions and stubbornness. They have natural glamour and film-star quality which can make them very attractive to the opposite sex, but perhaps because of their powerful need for independence they often delay committing themselves to a permanent relationship, and find it difficult to settle into it when committed. They are loyal, and make lively partners, both sexually and intellectually. The ankles are the Aquarian body area and must be kept warm, because their circulation can be poor. Children must be encouraged to use their originality creatively; rebelliousness must be directed towards humanitarian objectives, and stubbornness quelled. Science, literature and flying are successful fields for Aquarians as are radiography, all aspects of television, and social work.

Pisces

19 February–20 March

The glyph of the sign (♓) represents the two fish linked with a cord and swimming in opposite directions. The ruling planet is Neptune. The sign is negative and feminine, therefore introvert: its element is water and it is mutable, therefore Pisceans tend to be adaptable. Its body area is the feet. Its metal is platinum or tin, and its gemstones, moonstone or bloodstone. Its colour is soft sea-green, and its flower the water-lily. Its trees are willow, fig and trees growing near water. Its herbs are succory, lime and mosses. The foodstuffs it rules are cucumber, pumpkin, turnip, lettuce and melon. Piscean creatures are mammals that like water, and fish of all kinds. Its countries are Portugal and the Gobi and Sahara deserts, and its cities Jerusalem, Warsaw, Seville, Alexandria, Santiago di Compostella and Bournemouth.

In Babylonia around 100 BC the constellation was known as 'the tails', and the fish swimming in opposite directions were the goddesses Anunitum and Simmah, who represented the Tigris and Euphrates rivers. In Greek mythology, Aphrodite and her son Eros were startled by the hideous monster Typhon and leapt into the Euphrates for safety, turning into two fish. Later Zeus placed two fish, their tails tied together in heaven as the constellation Pisces.

Pisceans are dreamers; they may want to move in one direction, but often take an opposite route. Although they are the most sympathetic people in the Zodiac, they can be deceitful in order to avoid tricky situations. They are sensual and usually enjoy a rewarding sex-life. Piscean children must be encouraged to be truthful and be praised for artistic effort. The caring professions, dance, photography and artistic activities are especially satisfying for Pisceans.

Sources and Acknowledgements

The illustrations are taken from two illuminated manuscripts
Treatise on Astrology, Turkish, sixteenth century (Bibliothèque
Nationale, Paris)
Calendar and Book of Hours, French, middle fifteenth century (Bodleian
Library, Oxford)
Title page: *Les Trés Riches Heures du Duc de Berry*, French, fifteenth
century (Musée Condé, Chantilly)